His Words
My Pen

Volume 1
By Stuart Hardy-Taylor

His Words
My Pen

Volume One:
By Stuart Hardy-Taylor

Published by Little Nell Publishing

June 2019

First Printing: June 2019

ISBN 978-0-244-49056-0

Little Nell Publishing at The Old Curiosity Bookshop
116 Loughborough Road
Hathern, Leicestershire LE12 5HZ

www.oldcuriositybookshop.co.uk.com

Ordering Information:
Special discounts are available on quantity purchases by Bookshops, associations, educators, and others. For details, contact the publisher at the above listed address or email: hello@oldcuriositybookshop.co.uk

U.S. trade bookstores and wholesalers: Please contact Little Nell Publishing Tel: (+44) 773773-8018; or email hello@oldcuriositybookshop.co.uk

Contents

Introduction 5

Accredited to Only Him 7

At My Saviour's Feet 8

Belief and Faith and Saving Grace 10

Born Again..12

Christ, He Got Me First..13

Come Says The Lord 16

Faith Within My Heart...17

Father God, My Saviour Christ 19

For Him..21

For Us 23

Forgiveness Is Free...24

Freely Give: Numbers 11:17 26

Freely Slaved 28

Get Behind Me 30

God Made It...31

God Welcomes All 33

Gods Armour 35

God's Will...37

Grace 39

Guided...41

He Always Forgives 43

He Humbled Himself For Us 45

He Is Christ: I've No Need To Hear This Twice 47

He Is My God 49

He Sees Me..50

He Shall Save You Too 53

He Spoke To Me Today......................................55

He Was Always There..56

He Washed Them All Away................................58

He's Always There 59

He's Taken Them Away From Me 60

His Favour Down On Me 62

His Truthful Salvation 63

His Way..64

His Will 66

His Word Inside Of Me......................................68

His Words 70

Holy Is The Word 71

I Accept..72

I Am In Him 74

I Bow My Knee..79

I Couldn't Do It For Myself...............................81

In Him I Trust 82

In Him 83

In His Name Shall I Boast 85

In His Name 87

The Arms Of The Lord 88

Its Love Not Money 89

James 1 91

Jeremiah 33.3 92

Judgement Day 93

Introduction

Hello, my name is Stuart Hardy-Taylor and I am a recovering alcoholic/addict whom has been saved by the grace of God.

I was born into a loving family and raised in the town of Loughborough in the United Kingdom. As a child I went to a Catholic school and loved to play football and do all the things that young lads would love to do, but around the age of 12, I started to get in with the wrong crowd and it was at this time I took my first mind altering substance and my life would then be changed forever.

I was then thrown into a life of abuse, drink, drugs, underage sex, which would haunt every day of my life to come. Through the things I suffered as a child, I used substances to escape the restless taunting in my head from my past.

Drink and drugs gave me promises but never said that they wanted paying back for all the comfort that they would provide, and it was this lie that kept me enslaved. But in the end the promise of escape wasn't worth what it cost me.

My addictions cost me my family, home, job, and almost life and nothing in this world could stop my drinking or taking drugs, until one day in my brokenness I cried out to God and shouted "Please God help me I'm killing myself, I'm dying, can't you stop me drinking for just one day please", and he answered me and told me to go to a soup kitchen at the church up the road to see an old friend who had turned to God some years before.

I went to the church near where I lived and started to hear the word of God and how he loved me and sent his son to die for all of my sin, and that in him and through him, I could be free and reconciled with God.

I went into a rehabilitation center for my addiction to the substances that were killing me and it is here that God started to speak to me through the word and I found myself writing it out in poetry and through these writings my thinking and my life started to change and be transformed.

"I was renewing my mind daily upon his word" and this is where the title of the book comes from because they are
"HIS WORDS MY PEN"

It was the 17 august 2015 when I went into rehab coming out of a 32-year addiction, 32 years of fear, pain and lost, but most of all, a life-time of being separated from God in the darkness. But I pray in faith and hope that these poems will touch hearts and give someone somewhere the hope to reach out in faith that God will answer and transform their lives as he has done to mine.

May God bless you all and his peace and love be with you

Stuart Hardy-Taylor

HIS WORDS MY PEN

Accredited to Only Him

Who then but our god, has the power to tell the
creatures of the sea to live and swim?
No one but our god, for their birth is accredited to
only him

Who then but our god, has the power to tell a man to
live and not to die?
No one but our god, for accredited to only him, is all
life in the heavens, earth and sky

Who then but our god, has the power to command the
seasons here upon the earth?
No one but our god, for accredited to only him is their
beauty and all their worth

Who then but our god, has the power to take our sin
and purify us all, through the death of his only son?
No but our god, for accredited to only him, is the
power he gave to only one

Who then but our god, has the power make nations
turn to him and praise his name and want to sing?
No one but our god, for he is the power and the glory
and all that we ever are
IS ACCREDITED TO ONLY HIM.
AMEN

At My Saviour's Feet

Through my faith I receive his righteousness,
Through the power of his grace I am transformed.
Through his crucifixion did I die,
But through his resurrection am I reborn.
Through one encounter the fire in me was lit,
And through his wisdom shall I learn.
Through my love for him am I on fire,
Through my zeal for him, forever shall the fire burn.
Through his mercy I am forgiven,
And through his blood I am cleansed and healed.
Blind faith is how I see, and spirit led faith is how I feel,
Through reconciliation am I worthy.
Through the son's death upon this earth,
For me, Christ intercedes with his father in heaven.
And so, God my heavenly father now tells me of all my
worth,
So, I shall walk within the spirit and believe in what the
eyes don't see.
Because God spirits dwells within and Jesus Christ he
walks with me,
But in this world, I shall have my troubles, but I have
faith within the father's son.
For stronger is the one that lives in me, for Jesus Christ
has overcome,
And so, death you have been beaten, so now tell me

where's your sting.
And Satan; there was a party up in heaven, when I turned away from you, did you not hear the angels sing?
So, my soul is now redeemed, and you no longer have a hold on me.
For Jesus Christ my lord has is risen, he died to rise again and to set my spirit free,
Pray Amen, Jesus died for me and yes for me he paid the cost.
Satan; I bet you thought you'd won when you saw him die upon that cross,
So just as Jesus rose again, he brought me out of addiction and led me from my dark and isolated room,
He brought me to new life, he saved me from the darkness, and he saved me from your tomb.
So now when down and weary and I am feeling low and weak,
Never again shall I ever turn to you, for I shall always turn and face the cross and knee
AT MY SAVIOURS FEET

Belief and Faith and Saving Grace

Belief and faith should come together, and they
should be with one another,
For just as a child it cannot be born, without a father
or a mother.

For when belief and faith meet and marry, there is a
party in heaven above,
For then the grace of God is born out of his pure and
everlasting love.

Then Belief, faith and grace should live together and
forever go hand in hand,
For this is the will of almighty God and the way he
has it planned.

Belief and faith ignite us and through his loving grace
our spirits are born again,
And this is where grace and love show us that we are
the chosen ones and children of the greatest name.

Belief and faith are the cornerstones and without them
our walls shall tumble down,
But so powerful is the grace of God that his love for
us shall always be around.

Today I have belief and faith in name of Jesus Christ and my belief and faith comes in the knowing that he has set me free,
It is through my belief and faith in his death and resurrection that my God showers his saving grace right down on me.

It is only through my acceptance of my saviour Jesus Christ that today my God can look upon my face,
But it is only through my belief that I have a faith to receive his redeeming saving grace.

Born Again

Today the old has gone and the new has come,
Through Jesus Christ the saviour son.
I'm a new creation and I'm born again,
My Life transformed in Christ Jesus name.
Lifted up with him upon the cross to die,
Resurrected life and again within my saviour do I rise
Transformed and cleansed in the blood of the lamb,
Forever to walk with Jesus Christ the son of man.
Born again, a righteous man in a life anew,
I praise you Jesus Christ, for this righteous flesh, for
it comes through you.
And so no longer do I live in fear or am I tossed and
torn,
For in the name of Jesus Christ I have been re-born.
Re-born again and made anew to do Gods will,
He's made me a shining light and for my saviours
name I shall be that city upon that hill.
So here I stand as salt to taste and without blame and
guilt and hurt or shame,
And that is because I am a transformed man and
through the grace of God am born again.

Christ, He Got Me First

When we take Jesus Christ as our lord and saviour,
then at us the devils he's gonna fire,
And then the devil will try and pull us back and make
out that it is the truth that is the liar.
But today, myself I stand on the word of God and
when I'm being tempted it's his word , I'm gonna use.
So, if the devil wants to come and take me on, then he
better know he's gonna loose.

For I've taken Jesus as my lord and saviour, whom
has cleansed me of my sins,
And I suggest, that the devil read the history books,
because he'll read that against Christ, he never wins.
Three times he tempted Jesus in the desert but still
then he never won.
And then the devil tempted Jesus, with all the
kingdoms of world, but it was the world and all its sins
that Christ came to overcome.

And the devil thought he'd won and beaten Christ,
when he seen my saviour die upon the cross,
But three days later, when the father resurrected the
eternal king, then once again Satan knew that he had lost.

So I do not stand in fear today for I know the tempter
is laid down in defeat,
Because I knelt at the cross of Jesus Christ where my
sin and his righteousness came to meet.

So, I stand with Christ in victory and in his glory for
ever shall I rein,
And when devil wants to come and have go, then I'll
just call upon my saviour name.
For temptation shall not take me down, for devil has
no power over me,
For I am seated at the right hand with Jesus Christ and
in all authority.

But devil will always try and get me and at times
when he thinks that I'm alone,
But I'll just say, get ye behind me Satan, for the
Christ redeemer lives within me and my foot shall not
strike against the stone.
Satan will always attack me, with shame and also
guilt, but through Christ both of these I have none left,
And the spirit of the living God shall always walk
beside me through the valley of shadow of death.

For the spirit of God is power and in the word of God
there's might,

And no darkness shall ever overtake me as long I stay
within the light.
But the tempter of my past will always call me and
upon my memory door he will always knock,
But the love of God shall drive out the fear and his
word shall be my Rock.

And stronger is the one within me and he is the one
that will see me through,
So, tell me Mr Tempter Devil man, come on what 'ya
gonna do?
For my saviour he has beaten death and so in him I
am freed from within its curse,
And so, Satan, it looks like you've gone and lost
again because Jesus Christ, he got me first!

Come Says The Lord

Come to me those who are weary, come to me those
who are weak,
Christ says come to me those who are lost and come
to me those who are meek.

Come to me if you are burdened and those whose
lives are broken,
Come to me those who have fallen asleep and come to
me those who are yet to be woken.

Come to me if your heart is heavy and come to me if
you morn,
Come and receive the grace of the father; 'yes' come
and be reborn.

Come to me those of you are joyous and those whom
worship and praise in his name,
Come, knee and place your troubles at my feet child
and trust in the sweetest of frames.

Come says your heavenly father, come trust in the
spirit and the promise that he gave through his son,
Today, take Jesus Christ your lord and your saviour
For your saviour is asking you to come.
Amen

Faith Within My Heart

My demons shall never conquer me, my curses shall
never rise,
For I have the truth that I am a child of God and I
have favour within my heavenly father's eyes.
Lord, you have seen my sufferings, the darkened days
of my life that I went through,
I know that you were always with me Lord, but I just
needed to turn to you.

Lord, today I have my struggles, I self-persecute, and
teasing are my thoughts that I am always doing wrong,
But I am strengthened with your word lord, for when
I call upon your word lord; I know that I am strong.
My thoughts they often plague me, when the tempter
comes to play his game,
But I'll turn to you and pray lord, for the strength to
fight temptation and not to let the tempter put me into
shame.

But at times, I am frightful within my emotions and
my feelings; but I know within Christ I'm always safe,
So now never do I act upon my feelings or emotions

But I stand steadfast in my father's love, for in him I
place my faith.

In that faith that my god he always knows me, he
counts each beat within my heart,
And I have the faith to know he always loves me, and
never again does he ever want us apart.

For I now know that my past fears, emotions and
mixed up feelings, created the man I use to be,
But today I live with a faith deep within my heart,
that my loving God and heavenly father is always
Watching over me.

Father God, My Saviour Christ

My Father God, you set my spirit free from within my
soul,
My Saviour Christ, you washed me clean you made
me whole.

Father god, upon eagle's wings you make me fly,
And my Saviour Christ, yours is the name that I'm
lifting high.

Again, my Father god, on eagle's you make me soar,
My Saviour Christ, I heard you knock upon my door.

My Father God, you heard my prayers and you let me
in,
Oh, Saviour Christ, you died for me and to take my
sin.

Father God, I cannot believe that you chose me,
Saviour Christ, I can't believe you gave your life and
blood to set me free.

Father God, your love for me is so much more that I
am worth,
My Saviour Christ, I praise your name for my new
birth.

Oh, Father God, I'm at your throne and yes, I'm on
my knees,
And my Saviour Christ, thank you lord that you
intercede.

Father God, I thank and praise you for your saving
grace,
For Saviour Christ, it is only through your sacrifice;
that my God now looks upon my face.

For Him

I shall be a city upon a hill, f
or all the lost to know and see
And to show the power of almighty God
and the works that he has done in me

I shall be the shining lamp upon the stand,
To show his power of transformation,
Through his saviour son,
And spirits guiding hand.

For him I shall be the salt for the lost to taste
To show the truth and mercy in the fathers grace,
I shall be his message, his hands his feet,
And I shall be his promise as I walk the streets.

I shall speak his word,
and I shall be his voice,
I shall tell all the souls that are lost,
that in Christ Jesus name they have a choice.

And it is that same choice
That I made that set me free
When I heard Christ say, I am the way, the truth and
the life
and no one comes to father except through me.

And so now I shall praise his name and sing aloud,
and show the joys of my heart's contents,
For God's gift of life anew and abundant love,
And Gods sweet, sweet taste of recompense.

For again in life I can taste the love,
and feel in my heart all the joy,
Of being once again a loving father,
to my one and only son and boy.

So, I shall raise my voice
and I shall forever more rejoice and dance,
For my life today is a gift from God,
This is life reborn and not a new stab at life or second chance.

For he has taken all my shame and guilt,
My past, my pains and my hurt and sin,
And that is why today,
I shall declare my life, my love and soul
FOR HIM

For Us

Jesus never leaves us, Jesus is always there,
He's with us in his spirit he's our comfort in our
deepest dark despair.

Christ will never forget us; Christ never wants us to
ever be apart, His hand is ever on us his love is always in
our hearts.

Our lord will never forsake us; our lord forgives our
sins and all our wrong, His grace is never ending; his love
is pure and forever strong.

Our Saviour died for us and proclaimed, father my
life to you I give, He cried father it is finished, he gave
his life for us to live.

Christ died to be always with us, Christ never
sacrificed just because, He died for one reason only,
CHRIST JESUS, OUR LORD, OUR SAVIOUR,
Died for all of us.

MAY HIS PEACE BE WITH YOU,
MAY HIS SPIRIT REST IN YOU,
MAY HIS LOVE GO WITH YOU,

AMEN.

Forgiveness Is Free

I want to be free of my past,
So that freely I will live
But before my freedom can come,
Freely I have to forgive

Because the un-forgiveness of others
Is like a poison to drink,
My un-forgiveness of others,
Blackens my heart and the way that I think.

In my situations of past,
I have to accept and take my onus of part,
And find the room for forgiveness of self
Within the space of my heart.

The forgiveness of self and for all the wrongs
That I've done
Was the hardest part of forgiveness,
Which I have overcome.

And too in my forgiveness of others in what has now
past, and in the forgiveness of wrongs
Because forgiveness is freedom for all,
and the past should stay where it lives and belongs.

For the heart that forgives,
Is then a soul that's at peace?
Through the forgiveness of others,
anger and hate come to cease.

But my freedom has come,
Through the forgiveness he gave,
And through the forgiveness of sin,
Means that my soul it is saved.

And the forgiveness and grace
freely given to me,
Gave me life transformation in the knowledge that,
Forgiveness is free

AMEN

Freely Give: Numbers 11:17

The lord has taught me such a wondrous thing,
And in times of grief and woes his strength it brings,
For my Father God has helped and made me see,
That life today is not just all about me.

He has shown me that I can gain his strength
And stand up tall and strong,
If only I give freely of myself and recognise that
people's lives and troubles, they still go on.

If I can lend an ear or shoulder
Or just spend a little time
And bless their troubles with love, then the lord has
Promised he shall bless mine.

Just a text or chat from caring heart
Is all it takes,
And the loved that shared,
Shall give relief to both hearts that ache.

To remove self from self
And show another love and grace
Is where God can work and grant
His peace in that hurting place.

For the bible says that we should share
our burdens with one another,
For we are family, one body,
One Christ, Sisters, Brothers

For the message of Christ is
Freely love and freely give,
And when we follow this message of Christ,
Then we freely live

AMEN

Freely Slaved

As slave of God, I do freely be
And being a slave to God, means that he has set me
free
As a bonded slave, I give my life to only him
Now slaved to God, I'm no longer a slave to sin.

For the likes of me, God gave his son up to the grave,
So forever I shall bow my knee, freely as his bonded
slave,
No longer am I held in sins captive chains,
And sins darkened poison no longer fills my veins

As a slave to God, I do freely give
And as a slave of God, I do freely live
God is my lord and master and I his thankful slave
And I shall freely serve, for the price that my lord has
paid,

My lord he gives his word, his word shall be my feed,
My God he provides my all, he meets and foresees to
all my needs,

He is my God; he is my lord and I am his humble
slave,
And I freely give my life to him, for my God, has
chosen me to save.............

*Blessed be the love of God the Father, who's love
has no chains or burdens, no wants nor payments, for
what could I possibly give in return for his grace and
love and the gift of new life and I shall forever freely
serve his kingdom and praise his name, for all my lord,
my God has done for me.*

Amen

Get Behind Me

Get thee behind me Satan; get thee behind me
addiction and all your tears,
And get thee behind me Satan, for the perfect love of
God has driven out all my fears.

Get thee behind me addiction for my God has broken
off your chains,
And Get thee behind me Satan and tremble at the
sound of my saviour's name.

Get thee behind me addiction and Satan bow and
bend your knee,
For Addiction you are behind me now and see how
Satan turns and runs, from the one who set me free.

Get thee behind me addiction, no more shall I bow to
your powder drink and pill,
And Satan I rebuke you in the name of Jesus Christ,
as I give God my daily will.

Get thee behind me Satan and take your addictions
with you too,
Because today I live my life for Jesus Christ and that
is why, today I'm free of you.

God Made It

Man made the boats and the planes and cars,
But it was God who made the sun,
the moon and stars.

Man has made the cities,
which rise up high from out the earth, but it was God
whom gave this world its life and birth.

Man brought us electric, to take us out of the darkness
of the night, but, it was God whom made the darkness as
well the light.

Man made the wheel, with the tools developed by
man hands, but God made the oceans deep and the trees
and mountains upon the land.

Yes, Man made the medicines to make well and he's
also made the computer and World Wide Web,
But it was God who made the bodies the brains inside
inventor's heads.

Man created self and man created the poor through wealth and greed, but it was God who gave us grace and love and what this world needs.

Man has manipulated life for his own gains and has tried to make it fit,
But man forgets one important thing, that he's not God and life –   GOD MADE IT

God Welcomes All

Our God he takes the violent and he makes a peaceful
man,
Our God he finds the lost and gives them a purpose in
his plan.

Our God he wants the vulnerable and he loves the
outcast and meek,
Our God he lifts them up and gives them a voice so
they can speak.

Our god he helps the poor man and the rich man, who
is crippled by wealth and greed,
Our God teaches through his love and to show the
rich man, to give to those in need.

Our God he sets people free from their addictions, he
releases them from their jail,
Our God he gives them power and strength, through
every driven nail.

Our God he takes the sinners, who have killed with
gun and knife,
Our God forgives all those that turn and love him;
even for those, he grants eternal life.

Our God he welcomes all and it is our purpose, to tell
all,
They no longer need to search as, our God he loves us
all and all are welcome into his loving grace and into the
arms of his loving church

Gods Armour

Father God I feel your presence and know that you're
always near
But upon the days that I am drawn lord, I pray that
you hear my prayers.

For there are days when I am torn lord and by this
world I am attacked,
Father, my thoughts they try and tempt me, as the
tempter tries to pull me back.

But in you lord I find my strength, when in my mind I
find discord,
And my faith shall be my shield and you're spirit
shall be my sword.

When my thoughts are in the darkness, I shall bring
them into your light,
For the dark forces of this world lord, within your
armour I can fight.

With your truth around my waist, I shall feel no

condemnation
And no fear shall ever strike me lord, for I wear your
helmet of true salvation.

Your gospel shall be my peace lord, in the readiness
upon my feet,
Righteousness shall be my breastplate, so the evil
arrows bring no harm or heat.

So, I stand firm within your armour lord, for I know I
have your might,
In your armour I am steadfast, for I know it is not
flesh and blood of which I fight.

But within your armour I know I'm safe lord and
through your truth and grace lord am I free,
So, no more do I live in fear lord, for I have your
armour all over me.

God's Will

Some days when I wake in the morning and I feel like
I just want laze and chill,
These are the days I have to pray extra hard and again
hand God my life and daily will.

These are the days when I feel my past tries to come
upon me and my thoughts and emotions are trying to
integrate,
The thoughts of my past want me in isolation and
addiction and to stay in the house and procrastinate.

But I have to focus on my saviour and do Gods will
here on earth, as in heaven he has it planned,
Daily I have to surrender all that I am to the lord and
be guided by his hand.

For I cannot take my will back, for I would be in
danger of doing the things that I used to do,
No, I have to trust in the plan that my God has for me
and let his spirit Guide me through.

But God's will is not a burden, it is patient, loving,
gentle and kind,
For God's will only wants to prosper me to guide in
his purpose and leave my past behind.

God's will for me is abundant freedom, something
that I have never felt before,
And so daily I hand my will to my God and then God
gives me his promise, of a life in freedom forever more.

And if I have to spell out God's will for me then I
shall have to break it down,
The W stands for Gods willingness and promise; that
he will always be around.

And the I it stands for intimacy and the relationship
that he always wants with me,
The L it stands for life; a life as the man that he
always intended me to be.

And the last L it stands for love and of this love, my
saviour God makes sure that daily I have my fill,
And this is why I love my God so very much and that
is why I live my days and my life, by doing my
GOD'S WILL.

Grace

Now I am in his light, the darkness flees
and in itself it hides and cowers,
For I am under the transforming grace of all the Almighty
God, Which comes by the way, of his divine and
awesome power.

I am today, free of my past and I am freed of the scares of
addiction, Which I wore daily upon my face,
No worldly things could remove my scares, but today my
scares have been healed, by his empowering divining
grace.

He transforms the broken, the poor, the wealthy
and the wretched man like I, for free,
For the price of grace, did he himself bear the cost, of his
one and only son, for the likes of you and me.

He places his power and strength within in me,
to stay strong in my weakness and turn away,
Th empowering grace he bestows upon me,
Tells me that he sees me, worthy to walk with him today.

It is not of this world, nor my own human efforts that
have brought my woes to cease,
For it is the power of h is love, his word and comfort,
within his grace that has brought my saving peace.

No more shall I seek what this world cannot give,
And no more of this world shall I chase,
For this world cannot give me the things I need,
This world hasn't the power, of my mighty saviours
GRACE.

Guided

Guided by his staff and rod
Guided by the will of God
His path, his plan, is in our sights/eyes
His promise gave, our eternal lives

God/Christ is good for God/Christ is good
Oh, yes God/Christ is good
And all that we do
Lord it is for you

Guided by that all we've heard
Guided by his/the written word
His power is our strength and it is our might
He lights the way, he is the light

God is good/Christ for God/Christ is good
Oh, yes God/Christ is good
And all that we do
Lord it is for you

Guided by his loving hand
Guided by that all he's planned

His love is patience; his love is kind
He guards my soul and renews my mind

Chorus

Everyday he's guiding me;
Everyday day he's guiding me
Everyday he's guiding me
Yes, everyday he's guiding me

Every day he is my will
And every day he is my fill
Oh, every day he is my will
And every day he is my fill

Repeat

Repeat

He Always Forgives

Nobody knows, what my troubles have been
Apart from the lord, who knows the pain that I've
seen,
My life and true feelings I kept them apart
But my father in heaven, could see in my heart.

No one could see where my thoughts wanted to run
But I myself could not hide, from the love of his son,
And for many a year, I turned away from his face,
But Christ brought me back, with his love and his
grace.

I wallowed in pity and I lived my life in my woes,
But God planted his seed and through the fruits of the
spirit
It's nurtured and grown.

I followed the world and I chose the wrong path,
But never did he forsake me or show me his wrath,
And all of my losses, I brought on myself,
But now my life is in faith and my faith is my wealth.

I constantly did wrong, that made a sinner of me,
But now I am forgiven and forever loved shall I be,
I'm not worthy of his grace, for all that I've done,
But still he grants me a place, in his kingdom that
comes.

Never did I listen; I thought I was strong and so sure
of it all,
But still Jesus answered my prayer when he heard the
pain in my call,
I find it hard to believe he sees the goodness in me,
But he's granted me peace and life eternally.

He's granted me life, a life I can live,
To my lord am I grateful, for my lord is so gracious,
for
HE ALWAYS FORGIVES.

He Humbled Himself For Us

Our God he came and humbled himself,
To live among the likes of you and me
Our God he came and humbled himself,
to suffer and die as a man upon that cursed tree.

Our God he came and humbled himself,
Of whom we are not worthy too tie his throng
Our God he came and humbled himself,
But we exchanged his life for a murderous man and
still he forgave us our wrong.

Our God he came and humbled himself
For the likes of you and I
Our God he came and humbled himself,
In the form of Jesus Christ Our Saviour,
for as a man he knew he had to die.

Our God he came and humbled himself,
He came as a man to sacrifice his body and shed his
blood,
Our God he came and humbled himself,
For all the sick and meek and sinners and not just the
righteous, clean and good.

Our God he came and humbled himself,
Creator of all things, whom gave this world its birth,
Our God he came and humbled himself,
YES, our God he humbled himself to walk among us
here on earth.

Our God he came and humbled himself,
When he spoke out for our forgiveness,
The heavens and earth they shook
Our God he came to humble himself
And give man his written word within his holy book.

Our God he came and humbled himself,
When he stepped down from his throne, in heaven
high above,
Our God he came and humbled himself
For us and just so purely out of his love.

He Is Christ: I've No Need To Hear This Twice

Jesus Christ, the lamb the of god,
Jesus Christ the begotten son,
Jesus Christ, the sacrifice,
Through him, to the father we have become.

Jesus Christ, the king of kings,
Jesus Christ, the shepherd of the flock,
Christ he is foundation,
Jesus Christ, he is the rock.

Jesus Christ, he is the ladder,
Jesus Christ, he is the steps,
Jesus Christ, he paid our ransom,
Jesus Christ, for you that day we stood and wept.

Jesus Christ, spoke up for the prophets,
Jesus preached on what they said,
Jesus Christ proved the prophets true,
Jesus rose again, never to live among the dead.

Jesus Christ, is the son of God
Other faiths they refuse to bow,
And they refuse to call him Christ,
Jesus is the Messiah.

I know that Jesus Christ he is my Saviour
And I need not hear this twice.

AMEN

He Is My God

My God, messiah, Christ, my saviour king
My heart, my joy, my love, my everything
My north, my south, my east, my west
My work, my fruits, my deeds, my rest
My start, my end, my first, my last,
My today, my future and now my past
My sight, my eyes, my mouth, my speech
Your words, your love, your grace, I preach
My pains, my hurts, my rise, my falls
My wounds, my cries, you hold them all
My praise, my thanks, my songs for you
My strength, my guide, which sees me through
My food, my water, the air I breathe
You are the father that fills my needs
My lord, my shepherd, my staff, my rod
MY CHRIST, MY SPIRIT, MY LIFE
MY GOD.

He Sees Me

I'm praising the lord Jesus Christ on high,
For giving me life when I was ready to die,
For Christ pulled me free from the hands of death,
He gave me strength when I had none left.

Jesus Christ spat into my eyes
He said wake up sleeper in my strength you rise,
He spat in my eyes when my death was signed,
And he gave me sight when I was lost and blind.

For I was ready to go the depths of the lost deceased,
But Christ pieced my heart and gave me peace,
Now I put my faith in the one whose love transcends,
And he gave me hope in a life condemned.

He called me child and gave me love to keep,
He eased my mind and gave me restful sleep,
Now I'm strong in Christ protected by angel's wings,
To almighty God my heart and soul shall sing.

The Father, Son and Spirit, three in one, the Trinity,
Christ, he gave his life and blood to set me free,
For drink and drugs, they almost took me down,
But today, foundations are on Gods solid ground.

So no longer is my life run selfish greed,
And Living water feeds the planted seed,
His truth in me and in his name the truth will out,
And forever in his name shall I praise and shout.

I'll shout with praise from the roofs above,
For Christ Jesus name and the fathers' love,
His yoke is easy, and his burden is light,
I use the armour of God when I have to fight.

He sends his angels with harps and cords,
Bone and marrow are split by the spirits sword,
His name Jesus Christ is above all names,
Born Into this world is God's eternal flame.

The Lord of Lords and Kings of Kings,
And through his grace new life he brings,
Today I am saved for I have his grace,
And my gaze is transfixed upon Christ Jesus face.

Crowned with thorns and drenched in blood,
He came to make dead men live, not bad men good,
And for my life, he sacrificed, and he gave his own,
To put righteous flesh back upon these bones.

He took my sins and covered my shame,
He's transformed my life and gave me back my name,
I praise the lord Jesus Christ for setting me free,

And for giving me my life and my son back to me.

For he has placed the truth within my eyes,
He's renewed my mind of the doubt and lies,
He opened the door of my death row cell,
For Christ pulled me back from addiction hell.

And today I live and sing a different song,
Because through Jesus Christ, my God looks at me
and sees no wrong,
No blemish, no sin, no stain, no self, no dirt,
No lies, no fear, no pains, no hurt.

Today God sees the man, he made me to be,
For through my Saviour's eyes,
MY GOD SEES ME.

He Shall Save You Too

If Jesus didn't save me, how come I am still here?

If Jesus didn't save me, then who took away my fear?

If Jesus didn't save me, how have I changed who I am?

If Jesus didn't save me, where did I find my purpose as a man?

If Jesus didn't save me, how come I want to speak his word?

If Jesus didn't save me, how come I believe in all I heard?

If Jesus didn't save me, where have all my afflictions gone?

If Jesus didn't save me, why then is my faith in him so strong?

If Jesus didn't save me, how have my problems come to cease?

If Jesus didn't save me, then who granted me this peace?

I know that Jesus saved me

Because I prayed and he helped me through,

So, pray to Jesus my Saviour

And he shall save you too.

Peace be with you. Amen

He Spoke To Me Today

Jesus spoke these words to me today, my child your
eyes are opened, come now do you see?
Your eyes are opened up to heaven and the peace that
awaits you my child, is yours for all eternity.

Of you I ask for nothing, other than you be, who the
father intended you to be,
And only for you to love the father in heaven and to
place your faith in me.

Of you I would never ask for much and I would never
see you crawl,
Open up your heart and eyes to me my child and
among men you shall stand tall.

So, come and pick up your cross my child, follow me
to death and then you shall be free,
Follow me and live in my father's grace and his given
life of eternity.

He Was Always There

When did Jesus Christ my lord saviour come?
When I was broken and, on my knees,

When did Jesus Christ my lord saviour come?
When I was addicted and diseased.

When did Jesus Christ my lord saviour come?
When I needed more than just a friend,

When did Jesus Christ my lord saviour come?
When in my addiction, I could see no light, no end.

When did Jesus Christ my lord saviour come?
When I wanted too, but by myself I couldn't stop my
self-abuse,

When did Jesus Christ my lord saviour come?
When I needed guidance, purpose, truth.

When did Jesus Christ my lord saviour come?
When my life was truly hanging by a thread,

When did Jesus Christ my lord saviour come?
When my addictions and my troubles thought they
had me dead.

But then Jesus Christ he spoke to me,
And off my broken knees I rose,

Jesus told me that he was always there,
But the path which I had taken, was not the one he
chose.

So now every day I walk his path and I pray myself
his will be done,
And so now I know that Jesus Christ,
Was always there and never did he really have to
come...

He Washed Them All Away

Cleansed, through the Baptism of the water, He will take away the sins and all the shame, Lives given to Christ our Saviour, Lives cleansed through our Saviour's name.

With the promise of new life and to be taken away from addictions wrath, Reconciled with God the father and guided upon the narrow path.

Darkened fears will wash away, to be taken into his shining light, God's armour shall be upon you and the sword of the spirit shall be your strength and all your might.

Minds shall be renewed and with the spirit's piercing of the heart, Christ Jesus will be always with you and now never again to be apart.

The Lord shall take your past and grant you strength for your today, And have no fears for your tomorrows, for he has washed them all away.

He's Always There

I cannot see him, but I know he's always there,
I can feel his spirit around me, his presence I feel
within the air.

My hair it stands on end, yes, every single strand,
When I'm in the presence of my saviour and feel the
touch of his gracious hand.

In worship I sing aloud, in praise I'll raise my arms,
But in the presence of Jesus Christ my saviour, I am
humble still and calm.

PRAISE BE FOR EVER AS I KNEEL IN THE
PRESENCE OF CHRIST JESUS.

AMEN.

He's Taken Them Away From Me

While out walking with a new friend, he asked me
what my life was like before Jesus Christ came and set
me free,
He said tell me all about your life; please look into
your memories and tell me what you see.

I said I'll try and tell you honestly, but before I do,
there's something I have to say,
Sometimes it's hard for me to remember; not because
of the hurt and pain, but because Jesus Christ gave me his
promise and he took those hurts away.

So, every time I think within my memories and about
the pain and the power that I lacked,
Jesus Christ, he comes to me and reminds me, that my
hurts and pains are his now and that I cannot ever take
them back.

See I can tell you all about my past, but only in order
for you to know, that when I was broken it was Jesus
Christ who came to me,
I can tell all about my darkened days; but you have to
know, it was Jesus Christ who freed me from my prison;
it was Jesus Christ who set me free.

And so now I walk with Jesus, I no longer need to
look back and ask the question why,
For Jesus gave me the truth within my future and so
now no longer do I cry.

So yes, I'll tell you of my story and just how today, I
became to be,
So yes, I will tell you all about life and all about Jesus
Christ my saviour, who was the one who took my hurts
from me.

His Favour Down On Me

My god he created all the heavens, he formed the lands and
breathed life into the creatures of the sea,
But despite of all these wonders, still my god showers his
favour down on me.

My god he put every star up in the sky, he created all the
animals and the birds that live in the branches of the trees,
But despite of all these wonders, still my god showers his
favour down on me.

My god commanded the rocks to form the mountains; he gave
the order for the winds to blow over oceans and all the lands so
wild and free,
But despite of all these wonders, still my god showers is favour
down on me.

My god he came to live among us, he healed the sick, the lame,
the mute and the people that could not see,
But despite of all these wonders, still my god showers his
favour down on me.

My god he sacrificed his own blood
As we persecuted and mocked his only son and then we hung
him high, to die upon that cursed tree.
But despite of all these wonders, still my god showers his
favour down on me.

AMEN

His Truthful Salvation

If I hadn't listened to his truthful voice and I'd have
carried on in the worldly way.
Then I would not be giving you this testimony, which I
shall share with you today.

If I never acknowledge, my saviours truthful voice when
he told me of my worth.
Then never would I walk with him in heaven, or here
upon the earth.

And so, if I had chosen not to believe in him and put my
beliefs in my own minds web of lies.
Then I'd have been lost forever, instead of living in his
love that never dies.

And so today, in these words I hope you hear the truth, of
how it feels to be saved by his grace and tender love.
Which my saviour sends for all, from his mighty kingdom
in heaven up Above.

His Way

In the end, I knew was beaten and down trod,
Because all of my life I played at being God,
And because all I ever wanted to do was to direct and
run the show, but, in the end, even my loved ones didn't
even want to know.

By the end it was human pride that kept me on my
feet, but it was that same human pride
That took me to drunkenly sleeping upon the streets.

But then on my knees I broke and to Christ above I
cried, why all of my life; have I just tried to run and hide?

Why can't manage life and why do I find it so hard
for me to cope? And damn you Addiction and depression
for you have robbed me of my hope,

And I screamed and I blamed God -if you are there,
then why won't you stop these things I do?
And then with a voice from heaven above, God he
told me sternly, Stuart this has got to come from you.

Christ Jesus said; there is no solution or any cure or
wonder pill, If the sinning man, refuses to surrender and
stop living for his own self and running upon his will

For Man has always look to lay the blame,
For man refuses to take the onus for his actions and
then lays the blame upon someone else's name.

For the pride of man will not place the blame at the
foot of him, and for this reason I came to die for man and
all his sin.

So surrender your will and place your blame and
shame on me, and just believe that I died for you and rose
again and I'll set you free.

Listen to your heart for it is me who is knocking upon
the door, for I am here to pick you up when you know
you cannot take no more.

So in my brokenness, I looked to Jesus Christ whom
wiped my tears, and then I felt the perfect love of God
which drove away all my doubts and fears.

And although I have still troubles, and many trials I
know, in Christ I can make it through the day,
Because today I live for Christ and I'm doing it by
HIS WAY
AMEN

His Will

Every day the lord renews my mind,
Every day he makes me whole
Every day the lord he guides me
And gives me protection for my soul.

My father high in heaven,
grants me salvation and gives me my daily fill,
In addition, I know that I am weak within my own
strength and that is why every day; I hand God daily will.

For when I take my will back, my mind wonders and
from his path I start to roam,
But I now I have the wisdom and the knowledge, too
know that without God my guiding father, I could not do
this on my own.

Every day he lifts from my darkness; every day I
know I am safe within his hands,
For I have built my faith on the rock of his salvation
and not the grains of shifting sands.

For in him; I know that I am strong, and I am stronger
still, for I know also my saviour dwells in me,
Every day the lord gives a real life purpose; by
showing me the person that I am and who I should really
be.

So, every day; I will shine my light for Jesus Christ
my saviour; for he has made me strong, unshakable like a
fortress on a hill,
Every day I shall be stronger; for every day, I ask
Jesus Christ to shepherd me and guide me by his will.

His Word Inside Of Me

Every day I read the word of God,
Every day I need his word inside of me
Every day I need the truth of how I am
And the truth of how I became to be.

The truth being; when Jesus Christ our saviour died,
we also died with him
When Jesus Christ was raised from the dead, death he
had defeated and so he cleansed us of our sin.

For when I read his redeeming word,
I repent within my mind
For now, I also hear the word of God and now my
eyes are opened and so no longer am I blind.

In the beginning god spoke the word and so he
brought forth creatures, man and life,
The sword of the spirit is the word of God and Jesus
Christ he is the word our saviour and shining light.

The word of God shall reign forever and furthermore
in my heart; shall forever the word endure
The word of God is, forgiveness, power, peace,
kindness and the word God is love forever more.

God, he gave the word to us and the word suffered
and bled, for the sake of his father's plan,
For god knew the word had to die, so the word could
be raised and resurrected and placed in the heart of every
lost soul and broken man

His Words

To you I write these words, although I cannot claim
them as my own,
For these words are meant for freedom in salvation
and I shall spread them, wherever that I may roam.
Every day I thank my saviour, for the gift of new life
and this gift of poetry,
Every day I thank my heavenly father, for granting
these gifts to me.
I shall not ever take the pride but with great honour, I
shall always take the pleasure,
In the joy of spreading the word of his salvation and
telling all, of my heavenly father,s treasures.
For in the days when I was lost, I lived within the
darkness and not by the truthful words within his light,
But since the day I confessed my fears and weakness,
his words are now the strength in which I fight.
Before I was slave, to what the world treasures and
holds so dear,
But then Jesus came and set me free, so now to this
world I hold no fear.
So, within this poetic verse, I pray you hear the truth
and find revelation in what you've heard,
I pray that you do, to give your life to Jesus, I'll pray
for you to also live a life of freedom, in the truth of my
heavenly father's word.

Holy Is The Word

Holy is the word of God, which transcends power and
might,
Holy is Jesus Christ the son of God, who turns the
darkness into light.
Holy is the sword of the spirit, which cuts through
marrow and bone,
Holy is Jesus Christ who walks with us, so now never
are we alone.

Holy is the word we praise, holy is the word we
speak,
Holy is Jesus Christ who died for us and so every day
we shall bow down at his feet.
Holy is the son of man, our saviour who died upon
the cross,
Holy is Jesus Christ our shepherd, so now never are
we lost.

Holy is the blood he shed, when our saviour
sacrificed himself on that cursed tree,
Moreover, holy is the ransom, which Jesus Christ our
saviour paid for you and me.

I Accept

I accept, that I'm not all knowing
and I'm not all seeing,
And I haven't got all the answers,
for I'm just a man and human being.
But what I am today is a transformed man,
By the grace of God and firm belief in his perfect
plan.

See all my life I ran on self
and I only ever thought of I,
And it was that caused me pain
And my heart to cry.
Because through my actions never,
I did I just hurt myself,
Because I also hurt my wife,
my son and everyone else.

Yes, I sat for years
on life's pity pot,
And only when it was gone,
did I realise what I'd not got.
Wow, my wife and son had really gone
And still my addictive denial,
would not let me see myself in all my wrong,
Never did I ask or want to know the reason why.

For I chose to live in pity
and believe in addictions lies,
Today it is only through Gods power
And awesome grace,
Can I look in the mirror?
And see the forgiveness upon my face.

For I have come to accept
all the things that I know now are true,
And come to terms about all the things,
that I put them through.
See acceptance is the start and it is the key
For I had to accept defeat,
before almighty God could start to transform me.

Today is not about the guilt or about the blame
But it is about the fact that I'm
transformed man and not the same
So today with open arms, I
surrender all myself to Gods own will
For today I am not scared,
as I climb the mountains and not the hill.

But I had to stop the pains
and all the tears that all my loved ones wept
And so I went to my knees and cry out to god that
I ACCEPT

I Am In Him

For a new life and true faith to grow and begin
First, we have to believe in the word and that Christ
came to save and then to put all our faith then in him.

And we have to have the belief in the truth, that
through him the old it has gone and the new it has come,
And that we've been cleansed in our Saviour's blood
and been forgiven for all the sin that we've done.

See through him we have been released from our
prisons and he says that we've served all our time,
Yes, Christ says that we've been freed of our
sentence and freed of our crimes.

For he has taken our transgressions and the times
when we sinned and denied,
And he's taken them to the cross of salvation, so that
every day we can walk our saviour and cross and be with
him crucified.

It is here he takes all of our sins and in an exchange
for his righteousness,
Then the Holy Spirit starts to transform and then God
completes his works then in us.

So, let us start living in a life that is holy and at one
with the vine
and not keep reading the unchangeable stories line
after line.

Let's start believing in the grace of the father and the
daily renewing of mind.
And living by the fruits of the spirit, being patience
and loving, and showing forbearance and through all self-
control and also being faithful and gentle and peaceful,
joyous and kind.

And the life that's behind us let us not count it as loss,
for new life is a joy and promise for all at the foot of his
cross.

For through the cross and the grace of the father, I am
the man and father whom I'm meant to be,
For today I am present, for my son and mother and
father my sister my brother, and my whole family.

When I confessed with my tongue and took Jesus
Christ as my lord and my saviour and with the belief in
my heart, that by God he was raised from the dead,
It is then that I stopped listening to the lies of the past
and reading the book of the devil and the untruths that I
always have read.

For it is then that started believing the truth,

Of who I am in him, and who he is in me,
And through the spirit piecing my heart and healing
my soul, it is today that my spirit is free.

And In faith, mountains are moved and in size by the
smallest of seeds,
And all of my mountains have been tossed in the sea
by the blood that he bleeds.

But the blood that he bled on the cross, would break
the curse of death and the fall,
And Christ sacrificed his own life for our sins and yes
once and for all.

For god so loved the world,
That his one and only son he was sent,
And to die for all the sins of this world
And for everyman to repent.

And for us all to return to the father
And to his kingdom that comes,
But the only way to father, is through
the acceptance and belief in his son.

You see we need to walk in the light of our saviour
and feed on his word every day,
For the bible says he is the truth and the life, YES,
Jesus Christ is the light of the world that shows us the
way.

And to eternal life with the father, in heaven above,
Jesus Christ gave up his own life for ours, in the
greatest ever symbol of love.

So, let us start walking in his spirit and in eating his
word every day, as it is our daily bread,
Let us start praying and healing the sick and casting
out demons and standing on the word as it read.

And start believing it the battles we face
within the heavenly realms,
But never forgetting that we stand victorious,
with Jesus Christ at helm.

So, when the devil comes calling turn to Christ and
the heavens and sing,
And praise in the name of your saviour and shout now
death where is your sting.

And shout get ye behind me, for I am at one with the
father and by his right hand am I seated,
And in the name of my lord and saviour, you have
power at all as you stand defeated.

And I'll never fear, I will not run back to my vomit,
for I am no longer your fool,
For Christ Jesus has placed you below me, you are a
resting place for my feet, and in fact you are my stool.

And that gives me all the power of heaven and earth
and all authority,
To command and rebuke you and tell you to flea.

So when we stand on the truth his word and in the
light of our saviour, the lies of the darkness, to us are
unable to reach,
And I pray, let this poem be a message to all and in
the truth of the fact it is only in the strength of my saviour
that am I able to preach.

And to preach of the love of the father and the one
who he sent as a ransom to die on the cross,
Because Christ came for the rich and poor, yes, for
you and for me, Christ came for all, the least, the last and
the lost.

And so I stand here before you free of my past and
that is not just because of my removal of sin,
It is because I know that Jesus Christ is my lord and
saviour that is in me, as I AM IN HIM.

I Bow My Knee

It is all for his purpose and for his glory and plan,
And it is for the fruits of the spirit
And the works he has done in this man.

It is all for the sake of his name and that today his truth now I
can see,
And it is all for the undeserved grace, and his empowerment of
his love which he rains down on me.

And it's for his crown and his kingdom,
for which I believe, and I strive,
And it is through his promise and the power of the cross,
which is why today I am alive.

I believe in the transforming of lives which comes
through the name of his son,
And I believe in the promise of heaven on earth
and that his kingdom shall come.

It is for his guidance and teaching,
Through the Holy Spirit he sent,
And for the fact that I can now live in the likeness
Of Jesus, if I just believe and repent.

It is because he's made me feel worthy and
told me my worth,
Because he pulled me free from my darkness,
washed me clean of my sins and he gave me new birth.

It is for all the pain he has taken and the truth
that through his strikes today I am healed,
And for it is his strength that I fight in the seed of faith which
he gave me, which I use as my shield.

And it is for his grace and mercy and the fact that
I am not the same as before
And it's for his love that lifts me higher and higher and how
today upon eagle's wings now I soar.

It is to him I give my praise and my worship,
and I give him my fruits and it is all for his glory,
For it is he the one who is the author and director and the soul
creator, of my new life and my story.

And it is his power and his grace and his love that enables
me to do what I do,
If it was not for the grace my God and Jesus Christ as my
saviour, then I would not be here talking to you.

And it is without embarrassment or the worries of mocking
that I shout, and I praise in his name,
For I stand here free of the sins of the world and
without my guilt or my shame.

So, I here I stand in front of the world and I pray
you look and see how that today I am free,
And it is only to my God and my saviour that I give all the
glory and that they are the reason that
I BOW MY KNEE

I Couldn't Do It For Myself

So you want to know the answer to the question
How did I stop the drugs and drink?
Well here you are I'll tell you a little story, that might
make you stop and think.
I couldn't stop drinking for my sister; I could not stop
drugging for my brother,
I could not stop using substances for my father, I
could not stop, when asked and pleaded by my mother.
I could not stop using, although I knew the fact that I
was dying and that my life had gone to pieces,
And although I am a loving uncle, I could not stop for
my nephews or my nieces.
I couldn't stop drinking for my wife and I could not
stop drugging for my son,
And I couldn't stop drinking for myself and to save
my own life, when all is said and done.
I just could not stop drinking and drugging for my
loved ones, myself and all that I am worth,
It took something super-natural and that was my
death upon the cross and my resurrected second birth.
I could not even stop drinking for my God, because
my addiction would never let me be,
But when God told me about his son,
WOW, by Jesus Christ did he stop me!

In Him I Trust

I placed my trust in the father; I place my trust within
in him,
I placed my trust in his son to cleanse me of sin.
I place my trust in the spirit, for his spirits my guide,
I place my trust in the trinity for in them all I confide.
I place my trust in the son's death and Gods promise
and word,
I place my trust in the resurrection and all that I've
heard.
And I place trust in his church, and I trust and know
he loves me,
For today I trust in new life and the fact that I'm free.
I place trust in his power and for making me whole,
And I trust the word of the father, shall split my spirit
and soul.
I place my trust in the heavens and no more in drink,
powder or pill,
I wholly place my trust in divine transformation and
my surrender of will.
For I had to surrender my will up to God for new life
to begin,
For on the night that I fell to my knees,
And I placed my trust within him.

In Him

In the lord we do not hunger,
In Christ we do not thirst
In the father were never wanting,
For the son has healed us of our cures.
In the lord we are all saved,
In Jesus Christ, from our sins we are healed,
We are safe in God the father
And his ever love shall be our shield.

In him the spirit is ever present,
His blood for us he shed,
He died for us on the cross,
his body given to us, as our daily bread.
In Christ we have life eternal,
in the saviour we shall be raised,
To sit with our heavenly father,
far beyond the beaten grave.

In Christ Jesus death was beaten
And for the lord, never shall we cry
For in him we are ever living
And IN HIM our spirits shall never die.

AMEN

In His Name Shall I Boast

I shall boast in his name
And I shall boast without shame,
I shall boast in his plan
And all he has done for this man.

I shall boast in his peace for my sorrows have ceased,
I shall boast in my father above
And in his grace and his love,
And I shall boast that I'm free,
For that's what the lords done for me.

I shall boast with all that I'm worth
And for this gift of new birth.
I shall boast in the day as its long,
For Christ he died for my wrong.

And I shall boast in cross,
Where Jesus Christ paid the cost.
I shall boast in the blood that he spilt,
For my removal of guilt.

I shall boast in the day that he rose,
That it was me that he chose.
And I shall boast in his word,
And in all that I've heard.

I shall forever boast in the son,
and the father's kingdom that comes.
I shall boast in the ease of his yoke,
And for that day that I broke.

I shall boast in the day I was freed,
When he held his hand out to me.

For the love of the father,
the son and oh so holy the ghost.
My god is awesome in power
and forever in his name shall I boast

In His Name

The darkness shall not come against me for I live in
Christ Jesus's light,
Temptation shall not conquer me, for it is in the
Armour of God in which I fight,
Sin shall wash away from me,
I am cleansed in the blood of the lamb,
Death has no mastery over me,
I am resurrected with the son of man.
Though the devil tries to cheat me,
he tries to rob and steal and kill,
His lies shall never tempt me,
Today I live by truth and faith in my Gods will.

I shall not turn to my vomit
Or again feel addictions wrath,
For today, the holy one the son of God,
Walks with me upon my path.
I pray almighty father God, guide me in your truth,
and never again let me be put to shame,
And I promise forever and all my days,
shall I be praising
IN HIS NAME.

The Arms Of The Lord

Loved ones shall feel his comfort,
for blessed are those whom mourn,
Our spirits shall receive his peace,
in the knowing into heaven our brother born.
Father God, we pray heal up the broken hearted,
And bind up all their wounds,
For death here has no victory, through our saviour
Jesus Christ, whom has risen from out the tomb.

Father God we pray, you grant a peace that passes
each and every understanding, as we commit our brother
back to the ground,
And we shall wait in an expectation lord,
when the sleeping shall hear the trumpets sound.

Yes, Christ Jesus shall come again and at the coming
of the hour,
Our loved ones shall be raised in glory and eternal life
and in the promise of our Gods power.
Yes, we shall rejoice and we shall sing
Loudly and applaud,
But until we meet again great man of God,
Pray rest in the arms of the Lord
AMEN

Its Love Not Money

Some say that its money that makes the world turn
and go around,
But I believe money is the thing that helps bring it
down,
Man thinks that its money, that shall bring all the
things that he needs,
But money breeds self and money breeds greed.

Money don't buy love and it corrupts a man's heart,
Money is the divide that can force Gods children
apart,
Money can be poison and can cause pain and rot,
Money should not be the measure of how much life
you've got.

Money cannot do good if the greedy hands won't give
But money shared from the giving hand, can help
poor men to live,
Money should never make us different because inside
we are the same,
But money changes a man's feelings and brings his
actions to shame.

Money builds buildings that reach right up to the
skies,

But where is the money for children, who have no
food in their bellies and tears in their eyes?
Money is not evil; in fact, it can spread love, if there
is money to spare,
Money shows the lost and the poor that there is
someone who cares.

Money is not bad, money is needed, for us to live and
do good,
It should never be money that drives us,
IT SHOULD ALWAYS BE LOVE.

James 1

James, a servant of God and of the Lord Jesus Christ

Consider it pure joy my brothers and sisters,
whenever you receive trials of many kinds,
Because you know within the testing of your faith,
Perseverance ye shall find.

Pray ye let perseverance finish its works unto
completion, so that you shall not be lacking anything
within your maturity,
But should any lack the wisdom, then without him
finding fault, pray ye ask on God, whom shall give thee
generously.

But when you ask ye must believe and this is without
a doubt,
Because the one with disbelief, is like a wave upon
the wind the roaring sea being blown and tossed about,
For such a person is double minded and nothing from
the lord shall pass to you,
For within the trials and temptations they face, they
are unstable in all they do.

Jeremiah 33.3

There are questions that no man can answer,
Not even the wisest of men,
Within the times of our Saviour's church
No matter the lengths that man could go, for these
answers, a man is unable to search.

God said, call to me and I shall answer you and tell
you great and unsearchable things,
So, I call on God my heavenly father and pray,
for the wisdom of his word and the knowledge that
the word brings.

The fear of knowing his knowledge, is knowing,
But Gods knowledge, no man could entirely know,
But if I call on my father daily, then in him, my
wisdom and knowledge shall grow.

The unsearchable things that god speaks of, are the
things the blind cannot see,
For once I was blind and unknowing,
until God my heavenly father, answered my cries and
of my chains I was to be free.

AMEN

Judgement Day

I believe that Christ shall come again
and to judge man without reprieve,
And I believe that still, God shall mourn the loss,
of the world that didn't believe.

But Christ shall come again and in judgement
with a fist of iron
But only this time, Christ Jesus is not the lamb,
This time Christ Jesus is the lion.

Christ Jesus shall come again and to judge man and
all his deeds,
And the angels shall come in force
to separate the crop from all the weeds.

When the lord shall come again, there shall be
weeping, and gnashing of teeth,
But not for those whom are lifted high,
But for lost that's gone beneath.

For Christ he came before, to show he was,
the way, the life, the how,
And the bible says the harvest is ready;
The bible says the time is now.

The ends of times are near and for this,
the son of man was sent,
But only the second coming, is not for him to save,
but to judge those whom won't repent.

Christ Jesus shall come again and in
judgement on all nations,
Man's time has come upon him, in the decision, of
accepting Christ and his salvation.

For mankind, the price it has been paid,
Christ Jesus paid the cost,
For a man's sentence will be lifted, if he takes Christ
as his lord and saviour and walks with him to the cross.

For him judgement shall be passed and without
condemnation or correction,
For he placed his trust in the son of God and believed
in his death and resurrection.

Yes, man of the world, shall have to face the
judgement, of his sins and deeds of what he's done,
For Christ Jesus shall stand in judgement,
When once again he comes.

HIS WORDS MY PEN
Stuart Hardy-Taylor

L - #0099 - 050619 - C0 - 210/148/6 - PB - DID2535342